Letters To The Motherland

Robert Davis

First Edition

PAGE PUBLISHING, INC.
New York, NY

First originally published by Page Publishing, Inc. 2018

ISBN 978-1-64424-980-2 (Paperback)
ISBN 978-1-64424-982-6 (Digital)

Printed in the United States of America

Dedication

First of all, I want to thank my Lord & Saviour Jesus Christ for giving me the breath of life, the love for writing & the determination fulfill my dreams. This book is dedicated to Black people everywhere but those of the Motherland in particular. I am a person that carries the burden for my people. I want to see each and every person of color far from oppression. I want to see each and every Black person delivered from the strangling grip of poverty. It's true that most of us have issues wherever we are, but we're working on them. We live all over the world. We're loyal members of our individual neighborhoods, communities, states and countries, but Africa will forever be our mother.

I never want her son's and daughters to ever feel that we don't think of them because it's not true. I am told that from afar it may look like we're privileged, born with silver spoons, benefiting, balling, always eating steak, always in comfort and not caring at all about where we came from; but that's not true at all either. We know there are Brothers that want to but can't feed their families legally. We know there are Sisters attacked and violated by evil men on a constant basis. We know there are children who can only escape from the horrible pain of hunger in their sleep. I want those that read these pages to know we are not without our struggles either. I want them to know one more thing too. This book was for you! For them! For us!

To my parents, James and Joann Crockett, for bearing with me and praying me through all the horrific times.

To my spiritual mother, Mrs. Apostle Maxine Evans Gray, for never giving up on me or closing the church doors in my face.

To Mrs. Teresa Stratton, for listening to my visions and never letting me give up on them and also for being my printer when I didn't have one, transferring my handwriting into understandable literature for the world to read.

Mrs. Ammie Lacey Rayburn, for supporting my dreams behind the scenes, stepping in with support when I needed you and fighting the battles on my behalf I thought were impossible.

To Mrs. Jonell Brown, Mrs. Florence Gaines, Mrs. Martha Lucious, Mrs. Rubie Jean Davis, Mrs. Annie Lucious, Mrs. Pat Taylor, Mrs. Carolyn Moore, Mrs. Diana Sims, Mrs. Kathy Montgomery, Mrs. Nancy Rosell, Mrs. Agnes Heard, Mrs. Gail Roy, Mrs. Willie May Walker, and Mrs. Emma Woodruff, for not treating me like what I was, for seeing me, feeding me, believing in me, praying for me, speaking greatness into my life and giving me a place to lay my head when I was exhausted from the turmoil of the streets.

To Mrs. Camilla Virgil, for praying for and with me. Truly seeing my full potential. For encouraging me to keep pushing and making not only this one, but many more of my secret petitions tangible.

To the many Prestigious Brothers of the "Better Men Society" (state to state) who continue to fight the good fight on behalf of the people of our communities.

To the "Exodus Assembly", my church family.

And to the people of color all over the planet.

Contents

Dedication 3
Introduction....11
My Soul Is Stronger....13
Returned Empty....14
When Africans Sing....15
Shot By A Hunter 16
My Foot Is In The Water....17
Black Woman....19
Poverty 20
Everything....21
Locked Too Tight....22
Hope....23
Doesn't Stop Me From Walking....24
I'm After It 25
Finding Out 26
The Individual 27
Done To Them....28
The Tide 29
Never Had A Chance 30
Where We Live....31
Little Boy Black....32
Tears....33
Proud To Be Afraid....34
The List 36
Chocolate....37

I Never Knew 38
Wings 40
Perfect 41
My Own Weapon 42
Me A Man 43
Morning Prayer 44
The Fire 45
Ties Cut From The Beginning 46
I Go Fish 47
Our Numbers 48
I'll Change Lives 49
So Do They 50
Man Of The House 52
Happiness Amongst The Blood 53
Without Us 54
We're All The Same 55
Promise Of The Sun 56
Ghetto Ballet 57
Treasure Of The Memory 58
Missing Pride And Glory 59
Something Great 60
Black Girl To Black Woman 61
It Was Me 62
No Mother Or Father 63
The Way They Dance 64
Day Prayer 65
Child Soldier 66

Happy Pair....67
Today Being You....68
What We Have....69
Something Else....70
Same Mother....71
Not With A Weapon....72
The Lion....73
Not "A" But "The"....74
What's Important....75
Whole Community....76
Black Hearted....78
Our Ways....79
Iron Lady....80
On The Blessing....82
When They Mention Me....83
Growling....84
A New Day....85
Men....86
Our President....87
Bless Haiti....89
That Place....90
Imagine....91
Melting Pot....92
Our Leader....93
Black Male....94

Introduction

In these pages, I tried to really bring out the shovel and dig deep inside myself. I tried to make my brothers and sisters proud. There are plenty that can't speak for themselves. I hope I did them justice. I'll be satisfied if one Man draws strength from it. I'll be content if it encourages one *Woman*. I'll be happy if it changes one child.

For those individuals, take this as a sign that God hears your prayers. Every line came from my heart. Of course, everyone won't agree with every *word* but I truly think there's at least something for all readers. I believe there are even some poems that will shatter racial lines.

I'm not a gambling Man but I'll tell you the truth that I know.... my writing has inspired many to write already, but mark my word.... So many more are going to let their voices be heard after they see this!!! People that have NEVER thought about writing a book before are going to now! Lord if it be your will.... allow the masses to be moved and inspired.

Lord, bless each finger that opens it and bless each pair of eyes that grace it.

My Soul Is Stronger

They say I'm not supposed to be laughing and
In their minds I'm not supposed to be content.
They're confused I'm not embarrassed
for having pigment in my skin,
Thinking after all they've done
I should've got the hint.
I'm supposed to be angry and
not make a difference;
They want me to doubt my success and
come back down the Ladder.
All pissed off because they can tell
that I'm proud of myself;
And as I gain momentum my actions
make them even madder.
I know how the world turns
and whom they think they are;
But to my destiny I can say
that it means nothing.
I recognize that they are the people with
bank accounts filled up with money
But I am a person that's
always happy during the struggling.
I'm not supposed to be smiling
when they try to be mean;
I ignore it and stares get
cold and longer.
But I don't have to lash out,
I'll leave that battle to another.
and with my actions show them
My soul is Stronger

Returned Empty

Out of nowhere sprang captors my color.
Nets were thrown over my head as I watched
them chase down others.
Loudly I yelled and tried my hardest to thrash.
Hearing similar screams of kinsmen
suffering from ambushes happening fast.
On my chest I'm drug through the forest
and onto the sand.
Like thousands of my people,
hogtied and forbidden to stand.
Snatching up every flower and robbing them of
every petal;
Removing the rope restraints then replacing them
with metal.
On both hands, feet and around the neck
Are the iron cuffs placed and rechecked to minimize any threat.
Resentment from the Women and retaliation from
the Males,
As we saw chiefs and top tribesmen receiving gifts
and making sales.
Smitten by their guile and impressed by their
so-called powers.
Doing the dirty work of evil men with skin ten shades
from ours.
Each and every small boat was packed front to back and loaded
simply,
With brief trips to a larger ship only to return to the shore
empty.

When Africans Sing

When Africans Sing
The past and present stand in the mirror
It's evidence that all can never be lost
because with those notes they protect remnants
people wish to bury
When Africans Sing
Prejudice flees
Mouths, eyes, ears, hearts, and helping hands open
What isn't there isn't important
When Africans Sing
I forget about the ocean between us
And the language barrier disappears
We are one family
When Africans Sing
I'm so proud to come from them
And even prouder that all of us came from her
I feel connected
It's like I'm home
When Africans Sing
It's proof we did
I know we are
And I know I am

Shot By A Hunter

Naturally fought off diseases
that should've killed me
Crossed great distances for food
with no trees or grass to shield me
No more rivalries in my species
than it has to be
I replayed the same knowledge to offspring
exactly how I remembered it passed to me
Wisdom of the weather and elements is what I've grown
to trust
Braved the seasons year in and out
When others who grew with me weren't strong enough
Mastered the creeping sounds of enemies
because I had to
Memorized the footsteps of allies
no strain and I was glad to
My teacher was Mother Nature, and I learned
everything from her
Made it a long way then I was shot down by a hunter

My Foot Is In The Water

The land is dry and adaptable.
The fear of the unknown keeps me
from venturing out of this place of
laziness.
An island of progress is spotted
amongst the wetness but mental
relocation is unreachable compared
to small victories
accumulated over time.
Watched and doubted, movement
has to be self-motivated and all
benefits should be embraced like a child in
the arms of a strong Father.
Moisture in the sand keeps me
aware, and constantly reminds me of
what awaits in the deep.
I'm unfortunately up to my chin
in the stay.
There's no other alternative.
Some swim away, go there,
and return with good news
of the amazing blueness
But everyone doesn't come back
to share the sweetness of
success. Some don't even live
to tell of the disappointment of failure.

Predators down under are
fierce, ample, and bloodthirsty.
But I also have a hunger
for knowledge and accomplishments.
Their ability to breathe
below should mean advantage
but my ability to think solidifies victory
in the confrontation
My foots in the water

Black Woman

She is the vessel of creation's arrival
poorly duplicated.
Being the source of all generations
And the first fleshly box to bear a Male.
She is the living portrait of the
Mother of all that walk upright
She is the Origin of those that are human.
The starting point on the road to now
Undoubtedly leads solely back to her.
With skin and eyes of earth's colors,
she remains the divine creation without
Physical flaw or blemish.
She is the carrier of the hourglass.
The owner of the moon, the root of the strongest
Strand, and the ark of Eve's Tone.
She is that woman, the Black Woman

Poverty

Freezing is the entire when sleepy.
No clothes and holes in soles,
Only blankets passed out weekly.
For miserable is the way that pride keeps me.
Unattractive buffets by the tens.
The adaptation of the Women and the
Adjustment of the Men.
Skating through life's wind
Knowing the ice is thin.
Numerous situations on which continuation
depends.
Till it's my time, never getting rid of me.
Hanging on to the best of my ability
even though I've felt the rain literally.
I am the only boundary, no trembling,
Just remembering past and present fears.
Tears that evade all ears but near more
screams than a jail guard hears.
A few things only, all belongings in a basket
But it's not the world I'm mad with,
Like fights lost for actions drastic.
Must past it like a pop quiz.
Opportunity of the silver spoon,
soon will drop his, when the knot gives.
I won't, because I'm on the bottom
And I'll know what the top is.

Everything

All shapes, shades, and colors.
Hair of every texture and ether.
Every height, weight, size, and build;
Each attribute, bone structure, and feature.
Every language, social status, skill,
and occupation.
Every zodiac sign, degree, political party, religion and
every nation.
Every talent, ability, personality, and vibe.
Every right, freedom, answer, problem
culture, and tribe.
It doesn't matter if others don't take it serious
And they choose to never dream.
I'm encouraged to know we are
Everyone, everywhere, and everything

Locked Too Tight

Strong and connected, I've grown to respect it
People gone it affected, because it's lock too tight
Hanging chandeliers from the ceiling, that renounces all kneeling
Too most unappealing, long and locked too tight
For all that was deleted, what God gave, no trade, I greet it
I'm a descendant of how they treated, our own that were locked too tight
Locked too tight throughout all seasons, being ashamed would be treason
Love Ebony till I stop breathing, and all that are born and are locked too tight
Buried by rockslides and rubble, hoping our will to live never huddles
Together ending this struggle, minds blown by the locked too tight
Smart and sharp as a needle, in life we'll reach our steeple
As it is so I wish my people, shackles torn by the locked too tight
We should love nothing dearer, cherishing everything in the mirror
When it happens we'll see clearer, straight from the home of the locked too tight
Hard to separate a single strand, example set needing attention from Man
Until we taste sweetness of the Motherland and again become
Locked too tight

Hope

H.urt O.nly P.romotes E.mptiness so
We continues to H.old O.ff P.essimistic E.nergy
H.aving O.bvious P.atience E.arly it's never too
Late to pick H.umor O.ver P.ure E.vil or keep a
H.ealthy O.ptimistic P.osition E.veryday
H.ours O.f P.roper E.motion allow
H.umility O.utside P.ublic E.yes and
H.anging O.n P.rayer E.verytime validates
The H.eart O.f P.ositive E.xpectations
To some it is H.elping O.thers P.ortray E.levation
To me it's H.eavens' O.rdained P.osture E.mployed
We continue to H.O.P.E.

Doesn't Stop Me From Walking

It does not reveal my present situation.
My toes are always exposed and
the tips of each one are more important
to me because I don't have any.
But not having shoes on my feet doesn't
stop me from walking,
My heels have more responsibility,
My ankles bear twice the burden,
my journeys are not as comfortable.
But not having shoes on my feet doesn't
Stop me from walking.
I feel the rocks I step on even more.
I have to pay attention to sharp objects
And my soles are familiar with dirt.
But not having shoes on my feet doesn't
stop me from walking.
I don't wear the products of top athletes.
I will never do any modeling in or with them.
And I might not even win every race against
those that have them.
But not having shoes on my feet
Doesn't stop me from walking.

I'm After It

Knowledge is afraid to come near me.
I have an unbelievable infatuation for it.
I would even argue that I love it.
It has become my addiction and my antidote.
Whenever-Wherever I see knowledge, I go into
kidnap mode.
My mind is a steel cage inside an
underground cellar beneath a mental maximum
security prison with one way in and no way out.
There, no one will be able to hear it
scream to get away.
I must consume knowledge and I
will never be kept from it.
I want it to be all mine.
Where it is, I am and where it goes,
I'll follow
Holding knowledge captive for the rest of my life is my plan.
One thing's for sure, I refuse to
live without it.
It has a legitimate reason to be
afraid.
Because I am after it

Finding Out

We've been counted out before they've
even sized us up.
We're doubted before they know what
we can do.
We're underestimated before they
realize our potential.
We're dismissed before they even
have a clue.
We were disregarded before the contest
began.
And we're last to get the benefit of the doubt.
In not one of their minds do we even have a chance.
A battle thought to be won without
them ever sending out one scout.
I came to prove there's more to us than what's shown.
and to display to onlookers what we're truly about.
Us being greater than they ever imagined is another thing
that they made a mistake at and failed at finding out.

The Individual

When I do amazing things,
they excuse the fact they dislike
the lot and invite the solo.
When I defy all the odds,
they disregard the disdain felt
for the collection and they accept
the one.
When I acquire the impossible,
they overlook the prejudice held
against whole and they take in
the single.
When I grab hold of life's
unreachable, they forget the bigotry
exercised against the people and
they tolerate the selected
When I accomplish the unachievable
they ignore what they hate about
the color and allow the privileged.
And when I manufacture the
unbelievable, they dismiss what
they have against the country and
permit the favored.
Without an announcement I break
barriers, blaze paths, and tear down
walls for everyone identical to me.
Excellence is the syringe
And I am the needle.
We inject all of us through the individual

Done To Them

Being put here to give the world a chance.
Volunteering there, to come here, told of
horrors in advance.
No memory of where they came from and
here as children with no advantage.
Inhabiting our race, though we're looked
at as the lowest.
In fleshly bodies to record the neglect and damage.
Storms of starvation, poverty, genocide
and hate that we will weather.
Depriving faultless agents of time,
along with Destiny and Heaven
holding us down to make themselves feel better.
A natural enemy of Earth's royal
Daughters and Princes.
Assaulting, killing, oppressing my people
unaware of their real offenses.
Towering over all others that are in awe of
the mighty white tree that's less than rooted.
With a fate and sentence so dreadful
mercy would sneak in.
And without proof, it could not be executed.
The truth is that their crimes are the same
because in reality all of us come from HIM
So I keep in mind that
He is the only judge and
And what they do to us, they've also done to them.

The Tide

Activity of their intolerant Sun's pull.
Combined with the workings of their fear
riddled Moon when it's full
Removing others from the integrating
sands of the shore.
Plenty of room for the motion of their ocean,
coming back every twelve hours
wanting more.
Invading the land slowly with plans to
submerge and demean us.
With the imposing will of this liquid
ideology that naturally gets between us.
Reminded constantly of the differences we have
by the waves that were created to separate.
High and low returns of the blue, green
and brown; spiritual water evil sent to segregate.
The obvious disdain that they feel toward us;
Till this day most of their heart's hide.
Was the tide from inside that was a part of pride called
Apartheid.

Never Had A Chance

There are no obstacles between the
Tape and I.
It beckons me toward it.
Down waiting on the signal;
from the corners of my eyes I recognize
the focus of those to my left and right.
At the crack of the takeoff, my body
begins cutting the wind without
thought of repair.
My legs are longer and my stride
is stronger.
I hear the grunting of my opponents
getting lower with every step taken.
They try their bests to catch me
but they only see my country's colors
and my numbers as I pull away.
They don't care about the first spot,
they just want to beat me.
Anything to be better than me.
I have done them a great favor already!
Their push is harder because I am here.
But I am the fastest
and winning is what I do.
As always, they leave disappointed.
And they never had a chance

Where We Live

Where breakfast and dinner
have no meaning;
and the alarm clock is the
collection of starving babies screaming.
Where the eating utensils used by our
Children is something we created.
And the people serving us what's supposed
to be food, have no idea how long we've waited.
Where what's poured in the bowl is not enough
to provide relief.
For this wet mushy porridge that we basically drink
And need no teeth
Where Men have families and Mothers
have little ones, and no one has anything
to give.
Where we continue this struggle
Where we try the hardest
Where we refuse to die
And still, this is Where We Live.

Little Boy Black

Little boy black, confused with no clue
Wandering around wondering what to do
With so many questions he needs to ask someone
about being a Man if he lived long enough to
become one
Not even an idea of what being an adult really is
Searching high and low for anyone older than him
to give him his
One that helps him avoid being part of this cycle
Leading him towards a bright future and away
from the rifle
Hands-on in any situation he's in or direction he
chose to go
Seeking to provide guidance and information he's
supposed to know
Holding evidence in front of him of the success of
Elders that are wise
Along with reasons things are the way they are
and the difference between truth and lies
Not only telling him but showing him the proper
attributes to snatch
from the character of a good role model that also
has a similar face to match
Someone that recognizes young ones have big brains that need
to be fed
And deals with whatever's going on in Little Boy
Black's head

Tears

I cry tears.
For what my people endure daily.
For those that risked their lives and
left behind a baby.
For the ones that devastation did not avoid.
For those that remain after seeing
their homes destroyed.
I cry tears
For the parents that
couldn't protect their Sons and Daughters.
Events so overwhelming; with no
warning it comes and slaughters
For individuals of the family
that were too old and caught off guard.
For neighbors that were disabled
while everything around them got
torn apart.
I cry tears.
For the ones before and after
looked upon as sickly and ill.
For all that was lost
along with memories and physical things we must rebuild.
For every victim that died without a hero.
For those that had their own and ended up with
zero.
I cry tears

Proud To Be Afraid

Weaklings at heart not wanting to accept the crown.
Often associated with Africans being a reason they kept a frown.
Cowards caught between being ashamed and misled.
Bilingual and mingle with those with longer thinner hair in their heads.
Skin tones of variety from Ebony to Cedar.
Experiencing prejudice from every side, those they speak like not wanting them either.
Separating themselves from the Mother; claiming somewhere else is their ancestors' home.
But we know slavery brought us there, we volunteered to come, or magically migrated on our own.
Wanting to belong and being played like a tuba.
Because they were born or grew up in Brazil, France, Puerto Rico or Cuba.
The day oppressed, afternoon prohibited, and the night squashed.
Dark-skinned cultures being mimicked, adopted, and whitewashed.
Anglicizing is what they've done best since we met them.
Pale faces and pink toes imported to replace us, and we let them.
Labeled South American, Aborigine, Samoan, or Dominican.
Because their parents were Portuguese, Spanish, Israeli, Iraqi, Asian, or Indian
Hiding behind different languages trying their best to denounce the gift.
Fully knowing execution eventually knocks on their door too at the sift.

It'll be hard and the cards will never fall and stack
Equal.
Until we're proud of the truth; God made us different
nations of
Black people.
So for every Brother and Sister who feels that they're part of
the crowd that we delayed.
Can from now on be written off as "Spineless"
because we know that they're
Proud to be Afraid

The List

To stay
To teach
To try
To reach
Mentally feeding the ones to whom life has been the meanest
To instill Bravery into and give a chance to the next genius
To lead by example
To make sure the supply of knowledge is ample
To help the children in the nation
To ensure the up incoming generation
To provide or be a light, to improve our way of life
To show the world we can do it, to help my people
struggle through it
To make sure their time is extended
To use my ideas where God intended
To be who I am supposed to be, to never forget there
is a "we"
To leave the remnant and show the trace
To be there for those that have my face
These are the things I've found to be true
And what I know in my heart I was put here to do

Chocolate

Every continent is a store
and every Country is a shelf.
Every language is a wrapper;
Every flavor is the skin tone that we've been dealt.
Some were created to be sweet
and some were just meant to be bitter.
Colors from red, yellow, to caramel
and "us," the complete opposite of vanilla.
Different shapes and sizes ranging from
thin to the thickest.
But it looks odd to the untrained bystander
Why me and mine exit the inventory the quickest.
It makes the wisest ones realize that
despite all we must be the best.
Because spiritual eyes constantly examine
humanity and their fingers never touch the rest.
So never should we be saddened by our people
being graced by Holy digits and tips.
Because when it happens they go walking
joyfully back through the glittering gates that
represent his lips.
During our lifetimes we worry, doubt, & develop new
ways of trying to stop it.
But it seems like we'll always be the favorite, & get
chosen first because we're God's Chocolate

I Never Knew

I must admit I never knew the world
Could shake like the skirt on a hula girl
I never thought I'd live to see the day
That buildings would crumble and turn
my City Gray
I never believed that the street could open
and take away our hearing, running balance-
and motion
None of us were mentally prepared to
accept that these
Same people would fit the description
and be called refugees
Disgusting depicted what I saw and ghastly
were the things I was smelling
Blood, sweat, tears, and waste pollutes the wind,
blowing through these newly installed temporary dwellings
Cries of agony heard from the wounds
inflicted by the boulder
The feeling of despair on the faces of
every person even though the trembling was over
The lives of the first responders given but
taken like only the front seat could've
They stood firm and stayed together like
the steel and concrete should've

It was something we knew our enemies had done
that only forced us to be gracious longer
united and comprehended it was intended to
break us but fortunately made us stronger
Used a new unorthadoxed method of fear,
being diabolical trying to divide us
attempting to play God but only brought out
all the strength that he put inside us
I must admit I never knew the world
could shake like the skirt on a hula girl

Wings

They are what allow me to learn
When the words enlighten and teach me
Because of these sentences I am too far up for poverty to matter
And I'm too high off the ground for prejudice to reach me.
Because of these melodies and notes – I float;
above all attitudes that are ugly.
Because of my harmony I flap too fast
for judgment to ever touch me.
Because of my lungs I get to ride the wind,
and it takes me over waters.
Because of what comes from my throat
I'm carried to other countries,
around the world while crossing boarders.
Because of what comes from my lips
I reach for the sky.
When my mouth opens people from all over
want invitations to watch me fly.
I leave and go on journeys when I sing.
Because the voice I was given
is also a beautiful set of wings.

Perfect

Small perfect dreadlocks
and a face more beautiful than any other.
The coffee color of my Mother; because
her biological Father was a Brother.
Happiness and white teeth from birth she shows;
She flirts & glows & can work & pose
with her perfect nose.
In any clothes she's chose,
painted fingers and toes.
Brown eyes, thighs, and the size of the
round prize astounds guys;
Who'll flip for full lips and dual grips
on mule hips.
Facts lied about Black pride stacked wide
on the backside.
Stealthy to help me, broke or wealthy
she felt me.
Listens to Mr. Marley and sharply guards me
from the Barbie.
A smarty that's book tight,
Has never took flight and cooks right;
In my mind, this is what she
looks like

My Own Weapon

I could ball up my fists
and challenge anyone to a fight.
I could get mad, act out,
and go somewhere looking for the sharpest knife.
I could grab a stick or a brick
and try to make my problems run.
or I could lose control, go to the street;
and purchase myself a gun.
But I watch the mistakes of others
and I take heed to those lessons.
Meanwhile I'll fight with something else,
because I've found my weapon.
My brain is my fist
knowledge makes it ball up tighter with each look.
What's in my head is my knife
and I sharpen it more with each book.
What's between my ears is my stick
and learning more is how I swing it quick.
My intake of wisdom is my loaded gun.
Becoming more brilliant is what terrifies
and makes my problems run.
Once I've witnessed someone else fall in them,
I go around these holes and traps.
Constantly taught by the errors of others, which
are life's most available compasses and maps.
Point made with my selection,
I'll fight with something else. I've found my weapon

Me A Man

What makes me a Man is that I use my mind
I respect my Elders and I don't kill my Kind
What makes me Man is the fact that I'm a leader.
I'm a student of the game, a good listener and a reader.
What makes me a Man is that for knowledge I am a seeker.
and I don't use my muscle to prey on people that are weaker.
What makes me a Man is that I do not cross the line.
I know that I'm not perfect but don't commit any crimes.
What makes me a Man is that I refuse to go to jail.
and I'll find something else on this planet besides drugs I can sell.
What makes me a Man is my character and my Deeds.
and the fact that I won't make a baby until I can provide what he or she needs.
What makes me a Man is that I want to earn my own;
and I will not bring a child in the world until I myself have fully grown.
What makes me a Man is that I know why I am here.
and I will exit the scene quickly whenever ignorance comes near.
For what I believe in I'll make a stand.
Because these are the things that make me a man.

Morning Prayer

Lord, thank you for waking me up this morning.
Thank you for giving me another chance to do your will.
I know that you see my situation and how many of
your people are suffering. Bless us, Lord.
This tragedy happened but we know you're in control.
We desperately need an intervention & won't question
your motives.
You have allowed me to watch insects go about unharmed and I
know if you care about them, you care about us too.
I also know that you are merciful because you could've
allowed the enemy to take us all . . . BUT . . . You spared so
many and gave the survivors a chance. A chance to rebuild.
A chance to be saved. Lord, we were already in poverty but
the conditions in which we live now are even lower.
I have faith in your word and know nothing is too
hard for you. Heal us Lord. Mentally, physically,
and spiritually. Give my brethren a mind to turn
towards you. To turn away from crime, idol Gods and
false religions. Allow me to stand in the gap for those
that refuse or forget to acknowledge you and please
forgive us for our sins.
In Jesus's name, Amen.

The Fire

Reds, yellows, greens, and blues surrounding.
The absence of color giving directions
to every other.
The flickering of energy giving light
without being able to possess it.
It can't be extinguished.
Like the blaze itself, it has a divine purpose.
It consumes and is fueled by adversity
doubt, opposition, or negativity.
Only sitting stagnant can reverse its
systematic longevity.
It is the natural lamp resisting and
piercing the darkness providing warmth.
For those that are nearest
it's presence makes the time.
It's the moment of silence when wisdom is distributed.
The second when imaginations are activated.
It is the smoke signal in the distance.
Both useful and dangerous contained
by my flesh.
It is me and I am it.
It is the Black fire within

Ties Cut From The Beginning

Before anyone else, there was us.
Now we don't communicate and it's
each other that we don't trust.
Two separate halves of a single energy.
Both feeling let down, thinking
the counterpart is the enemy.
Blocked and deterred by the same nemesis.
Angrily pointing
fingers about who's the blame
since Genesis.
Holding each other accountable
for transgressions, and each
desiring what they've done to be
pardoned.
Infinite variations of the
back and forth arguing about
the different mistakes made
in the Garden.
Outsiders can see and immediately tell
that there is obvious animosity between
the Black Male and Female.
Visions with eyes open and shut have seen us winning.
But we have to repair and put back the
spiritual ties that were cut from the beginning

I Go Fish

I don't spy on a stranger's rod in the water . . .
waiting quietly to see what bites.
Nor do I sit in darkness debating myself
whether I'll rob his reel when the time is right.
I was taught twenty times that taking what's not
mine for ANY REASON is wrong and rude.
Also, that "bringing home the bacon" has to do with
you providing a lot more than just some food.
So I never allow myself to become tempted to
sneak a peek at what's on my neighbor's line
or creep up when their back is turned and they're vulnerable
leaving with what they've accumulated like its
mine.
I don't hover or circle covetously paying attention
to what someone else will catch
for dinner.
And afterwards come to claim
the trophy holding my head up like
I'm a winner.
I don't stand on the bank smelling and looking.
then like a greedy animal get as close as possible
while trying to snatch what's cooking.
When my stomach growls or my
family needs a dish.
I Man up, I get my bait, I get on
the boat and I go fish.

Our Numbers

It's not impossible and we're
already on the brink.
Of our people vanishing off the
earth entering a category called
"extinct."
Imagine individuals of all colors
being displayed in museums.
As a result of our family tree missing the
roots, fruit, leaves, and the limbs.
Now anyone can see we're dying faster than
any other race that's on the planet.
The reason being we're nonchalant about what's happening
And are caught not caring about the damage.
We storm out of the realm of complete independence
and enter the grim dimension
that slaves, serves, entertains, and pleases.
Doing to ourselves all the evil things others are afraid to.
Plus we're overwhelmed by poverty,
drugs, and diseases.
Ethnic cleansing, gang violence, civil
wars and disaster.
Animal attacks, natural causes, and
being executed by pirates that think
they're our masters.
We've given this country and the world completely
too many wonders.
for us to accept annihilation
from being lazy and totally neglecting "Our Numbers."

I'll Change Lives

If I can't change it for my Mother,
I'll change it for my Sister.
Stuffing my head with knowledge,
working till my hands get a blister.
If I can't change it for my Father,
I'll change it for my Brother.
By going to college returning with wisdom
and showing Africa how much I love her.
If I can't change it for my family,
I'll change it for my people.
Become a brilliant professor and get
an occupation that helps us become
technologically equal.
If I can't change it for my village,
I'll change it for my country.
And learn about vegetation so no one
on the entire continent is hungry.
I'll be somebody special because
inside I have the drive.
I'm small now but one day I'll
Change Lives

So Do They

I have nothing, I'm in despair,
I'm battered and I need a nurse.
But then as bad as it is it's unbelievable that some
of my people still have it worse.
I live in conditions I didn't think
a human could survive.
But as I look across the ocean
they show me the real meaning
of deprived.
We have been given a "taste" of
what they experience daily.
We have access to hospitals and clinics,
but for them seeing a doctor
is a huge "maybe".
Our home has been impacted
and we have shed a million tears.
But in the Mother Land they've
lasted through chaos like this
four hundred years
Not taking away from what
we're bearing.

But the stories of their neglected
and unprotected are still worth
sharing.
Horror and nothing less
can describe what my
family feels.
But what can be said about
them being invaded and
watching loved ones getting
shot and killed?
We are united by the skin
and our problems won't just
go away.
Yes, it's true we need aid and assistance,
But so do they

Man Of The House

I am the Man of the house.
They depend on me to provide
I must do something full grown,
even though I'm still a child
on the outside.
I'm supposed to be too young
to have these things on my mind.
It's my responsibility to somehow make money
without ever committing a crime.
I don't have many options.
It's true, I'm strong but nowhere near old.
I'm horribly under paid and
Often deal with abuse that most would consider cold.
I have to keep trying and can't
accept defeat.
It's the reality that I live in.
If I don't work, then They Don't Eat

Happiness Amongst The Blood

Still laughing after seeing so much death.
Playing around the violence quietly watching people
take their last breaths.
Locating joy inside even though their lives might
be in danger.
Innocent at heart, thinking no one means them harm
and no one is a stranger.
The stench of rigor mortis is far from
out of the ordinary.
And the fact that it doesn't bother them is
nothing short of scary.
Only babies physically but forced to be mental
adults witnessing the warring.
Unphased at the second, with no hint of what
these underdeveloped brains & innocent consciences are storing.
We'll know later what particular seeds were
planted
by the flower that comes from the bud.
but right now it's still amazing that any of
these children can find, momentary Happiness Amongst The Blood

Without Us

Attempting to erase our contributions.
Took what we taught them to the next level.
Wanting to blot out our names from the record.
and throwing piles of dirt on our deeds with a shovel.
Capitalized with all of their craftiness,
wishing to replace us in paragraphs of ancient text.
Cunningly pacifying our rightful place with a white pillow,
with common sense warning us they'll bring out the
blankets next.
Distributing our achievements amongst all the countries closest.
When they're not supposed to be an accomplice in the theft.
Giving them reasons to continue their deceit.
Bad neighbors being part of the lie and taking the credit for self.
Burning papers and scrolls that would tell the truth.
Feeling good inside being history's crooks.
Rewriting what they can and tainting the knowledge,
because they're intentionally controlling what's allowed in the books.
We willingly send our children to schools that are public,
Hoping each of their teachers are people that we can trust.
To show every Black student that they can be whatever they choose
and let the world see it wouldn't be the same without us

We're All The Same

We are all the same.
Arms, legs, heart, tongue, brain
and lots of veins.
Eyes, ears, nostrils, and lips.
fingers, toes, nails, and tips.
Shirts go on overhead and
pants one foot at a time.
All the same necessary five senses
and all of us having to use our minds.
Each of us has a chance to put
good things in the vessel.
Everyone with different talents
and gifts that make us special.
All of us can stand up and go past what's expected.
and take our time making decisions so the
proper choice & option can be selected
Not one of us should have a reason to ever be sorry
we came.
None of us were born supreme.
Black, brown, red, yellow, white
We're all The Same

Promise Of The Sun

As long as it rises there is hope.
Long as it does it's job there's a chance.
As long as it shines bright there is time.
I feel that as long as it shows, I can make a stance.
In my heart I know that all doors are open for me.
And as long as it appears as our source of heat.
I'm encouraged and I know that the battle isn't over.
and it's arrival is proof that the verdict isn't defeat.
As long as it's meant to provide us with warmth.
I know that my life isn't finished.
I know I have reason to keep my chin up.
As long as the rays of its light haven't diminished.
I know and believe the war can be won.
Meanwhile I hang on to the proof of the Promise of The Sun.

Ghetto Ballet

Wearing torn slippers with my toes
almost bursting through them.
Scorned but born to perform
twists and turns better than they do them.
To those that are privileged, It's a pasttime
but I point and lift like it's my last time.
Practicing pirouetting in garments that fit like skin.
mastering graceful routines choreographed
for the thin.
Constantly corrected in the mirror with
my leg a top the bar.
Taking negative criticism, having dreams of
becoming a star.
My motion imitating the flight of
an eagle.
A graceful gift
Not on the list of things attributed
to my people.
Dancing freely through the dust of
my village night and day.
I am a member of the Black African Ghetto Ballet.

Treasure Of The Memory

It's my duty to learn of my past.
I'm not whole until I know my history.
Finding out all that my bloodline ever did.
Each lasting known period of mystery
I was born and meant to uncover who we were.
I'm obligated to visit where I came from.
It's definitely good when I unveil things
about my ancestors.
The people and places we got our names from.
I'm doing the right thing to take my shovel.
Going back to dig deep in time.
I'm performing a service when I inquire
about them,
and hold the Treasure Of The Memory in mind.

Missing Pride And Glory

Thirst is not the only beast that lures.
All dry mouthes to the water that's as filthy
as old sewers.
Hunger is the monster that cripples the
population.
Bringing villages & cities to their knees,
While growling stomachs stop the nation.
Disease is the ghost that has the need
to haunt us
Giving steam to the train
saying "The world doesn't want us."
Corruption is the ghoul screaming
"I'm after their spirit."
But we're hateful, unforgiving, and too
overwhelmed with grudges to hear it.
Low self-esteem is the demon that
our people must face.
To bring back the pride and glory that
once was felt amongst the Race.

Something Great

I want to read more books than
anyone ever has.
I want to be watched by millions patiently performing
a difficult task.
I want to bring forth the tallest structures my
Country has ever seen.
I want to build and name the hospital my people see
in their dreams.
I want to change my city.
And somehow show its beauty.
I want to become something they thought I couldn't,
go back and do something for those people that
knew me.
I want to make it different for every boy and girl.
not only where I live but across the world.
I want to expand my mind and be a credit to my
Home.
and have whatever I've done to remain when I'm gone.
I want to design, blue print, manufacture and
create.
I want to be something magnificent & do Something Great.

Black Girl To Black Woman

I am smart and I am strong.
No recognized Royal family just makes me a Princess
without a throne.
I am determined to get where
I'm going.
I can do anything I choose to
because half of the battle is knowing.
I respect myself and demand
the same from others.
I won't accept being treated lesser
by any Man including my Brothers.
My spirit is unique and it has the ability to summon.
The resilience of the Black girl
and the brilliance of the Black Woman.

It Was Me

I know the way to make them die fast.
Let's see how many Brothers and Sisters
we'll smash!
It's true that these people all call this land Mother;
but this white skin and these blue eyes
can quickly make them turn on each other.
I'll find differences between them
By making one superior and by treating that one better.
You wouldn't believe that they'll be more racist
than I would and follow all of my directions to the letter.
Those left out on the bottom will see their
counterparts as traitors;
They'll get the hardest jobs, and who we choose
will be cooks, hosts and waiters.
They'll still be less than nothing to us,
but will feel socially above the hard workers just a notch.
This process will make them hate each other to the point
that all we'll have to do is relax, sit back and watch.
Put pennies and crumbs in the hands of the privileged
and let the ones underneath hold less.
Then after promoting two different labels
and suggesting they start a war,
It won't take long for them to forget that I started this whole mess!
After that, we'll leave the scene all together,
Like finally they've all been set free.
Then they'll fight five decades before they
even come to the realization.
That who was really killing from the beginning was me!

No Mother Or Father

I can't do any complaining, crying, and sniffling;
because I'm a child myself and have to take
care of my siblings.
Entirely too small to do a lot of things for myself
but I'm all my little Sister and Brother have left.
I go out and come back and have worked my body
through and through;
because my parents spirits are in me and if
they were here, this is exactly what they would do.
Finding them clothes, trying my best to keep them clean;
hugging and rocking them back to sleep when they're
disturbed or have had bad dreams.
There's no need to worry about the grumbling of my tummy;
when there are those that are smaller than me that are hungry.
I give them the mixture that the outsiders send me.
Plus I travel to the landfill and break six bricks for a penny.
I don't let my size or my tiny legs fail me.
I'll keep going and doing what my instincts tell me.
I can't sit and wait for someone else to bother.
I'm young but have to step forward because we don't have
a Mother or Father.

The Way They Dance

Dreams sound off from the hands that beat them.
Villages composed of the bodies of different families creating
an arena to greet them.
No shoes and dressed traditionally;
Movements distributed medicinally.
Cheerful noises from every seat;
jumping and stomping of the feet in the heat.
Limbs expressing the story;
of triumph, honor and glory.
Rhythm installed in the blood;
Freely and without being judged.
Coordinated and rehearsed;
known for the energy of each one's exerts.
Arresting from the first glance;
describes the way Africans dance.

Day Prayer

Lord, where I live is chaotic and I know you see.
Help me throughout my day today. Shield me from
trouble and the wrong crowd. Thank you for giving me a chance
to do the right thing. Bless my family, friends, and
neighbors. Introduce yourself to those that don't
know you and your greatness. Grant them repentance and
show them the mercy only you can.
Bless my
country Lord. Drive out genocide, corruption,
disease, poverty, and ignorance from our presence.
Allow us to rebuild our homes and cities. Restore us
to where we were in the world if it be in your plan.
Give us a chance to earn a NEW position and to reach a
NEW plateau. Allow us to do your will.
Forgive us for our sins, in Jesus's name I pray,
Amen

Child Soldier

I didn't have a choice, no one could hear my voice.
A child that was wild, seeing bodies in piles.
I didn't want to do bad things
Or witness the carnage the militia brings.
I was forced to go along with the fighting;
And unaware of the hatred we were igniting.
Without them caring if it would mentally derail me.
I was sent to kill for reasons they'd never tell me.
No one to run to and nowhere to turn.
What to shoot and burn is what I've learned.
I was there and remember too many details.
About violence, rapes, mutilation and murders
done to females.
Robbing villages and torching crops.
Involved in a grudge that never stops.
I was introduced to drugs and only spent
A little while sober.
I was plucked from my home and changed
into a child soldier.

Happy Pair

Years together, that fears forever
When my mind plays it back
It's in divine shades of black
The perfect couple that works the muscle
With any curse we tussle because we birthed the hustle.
The very idea of us sings and cheers between the ears
Paying attention and listening
Staying to mention the whistling
I'm a Male that doesn't wait
to scrape what's on the plate
Not a single thump is what we give rage
From the red object beating behind the rib cage
We both come from a good pedigree
that guides and goes ahead of me steadily.
Not concerned with my own longevity
Whatever's wrong, I'm here to get
Rid of it, by being considerate
I choose to be with who's for me
We are the Happy pair with Nappy hair

Today Being You

Children that don't seize the chances
Chances to change the world and
become someone
Someone we read about in the books
Books we learn from in Schools
Schools that try to teach us
Us, the people that are deprived
Deprived of knowledge on their level
The level of equality
Equality for whites and Blacks
Black students of the second
The Second being the open window
The Window into the house
The house being time's present
The present, past, and future
The Future being tomorrow
Tomorrow is what's left when now is gone
Gone meaning no more today
Today being you

What We Have

If we aren't thankful for the lesser;
We won't appreciate the greater.
If we can't handle the minor;
Then we can't manage the major.
We won't hold on to what's big;
If we aren't clinging to what's small.
If we are only slightly glad about the tiny;
The enormous won't make us happy at all.
If we can't defend the little;
Then we can't protect a lot.
If you can't maintain a single sheep;
Then the same can be expected for the flock.
There are always blessings in store for us to grab;
But first we must cherish what we
already have.

Something Else

We've seen our people;
What they've suffered
and what they've endured.
The effects of starvation
and minor diseases that
go uncured.
We've seen our people
killing one another and
murdering each other daily.
Alienating the innocent;
destroying the future of defenseless babies.
We've seen our people
burn food supplies
and use war as an excuse;
For killing so many Black humans
without using the white hood
or noose.
We've seen our people
argue, fight, fuss and be
out for self.
Now it's time for all of
us to see our people on another level doing something else.

Same Mother

Libya, Egypt, Chad, and South Sudan;
Algeria, Morocco, Mali, and Ghana.
South Africa, Namibia, Congo, Zimbabwe,
Mozambique, Tanzania and Botswana.
Reunion, Swaziland, Madagascar, and Lesotho;
Burkena Furso, Seychelles, Mauritius, and Togo.
Somalia, Central African Republic, Sudan, Malawi, and Uganda;
Gabon, Comoros, Angola, Kenya, Ethiopia, and Rwanda.
Eritrea, Ivory Coast, Democratic Republic of Congo and Liberia;
Sierra Leone, Guinea, Mauritania, and Nigeria.
Tunisia, Cameroon, Cape Verdi, Benin and Gambia;
Senegal, Niger, Djibouti, Burundi, and Zambia.
It's no secret that each other's backs we should have and cover.
The reason is because we all live on, benefit
from and came from the Same Mother.

Not With A Weapon

Blood spilled in the dust
doesn't make life better for us.
Letting go rounds when your finger squeezes;
doesn't delete any of these diseases.
Being a part of a gang or militia that allows this;
Will never give us better houses.
Soldiers lined up in front of me;
Will never stimulate the economy.
A nine's range, will never make minds change.
Holding an A-K, won't give hard workers a payday.
Packing an extra clip, won't make poverty loosen its grip.
Giving a rifle to those with rage
won't help our children get better grades.
Being the devil's advocate, can't
raise the number of College graduates.
Throwing grenades from the hand.
Won't help us re-cultivate our land.
War paint on our faces, won't get rid of all the racists.
Violence against those that live locally
won't put us where we should be socially.
Covert operations undercover
won't make us love each other.
The practice of tyranny
won't assure every ear is hearing me.
Progress will be made when we learn this lesson.
Because none of our problems can be solved With A Weapon.

The Lion

It's mind, it's teeth, it's size, it's claws.
It is the abomination roaming
the jungle that is society.
Hungry for the sweet meat of competition
of any kind.
Challengers come one, come all.
It is larger, stronger, faster, and fiercer
than its Golden haired counterparts so it
is always kept separate from them.
It is the original and the destroyer of the new king of beasts.
It's roar alone buckles them.
It is given a designated domain
for it's Claws and Mane
away from the others.
It is made to stay where there are only lions like it.
Where it can only kill it's own kind.
We must not only keep them contained and
away from any other felines, but we have to keep it away
from other animals period!
We must make them each other's only visible adversary.
We have to pin them in and starve them out.
They must also be each other's only possible food source.
the mortality, longevity and survival of the top meat eater's at stake
and it should not have to compete with this monster.
One of them may stray into the territory of the preferred
big cats but it will be outnumbered and at a
disadvantage.
They can't be allowed to overrun the others.
These are no regular Lions.
These are Black Lions.

Not "A" But "The"

I am not "A" Black girl. I am "the" Black girl.
I am the Black girl that will not give up on herself;
The Black girl that will exceed expectation.
The Black girl that will not get distracted;
The Black Girl that will get her education.
The Black Girl that realizes her God-given potential;
The Black Girl that will shine the brightest.
The Black girl that will not stop studying;
The Black girl that will score the highest.
The Black girl that will not get pregnant early;
The Black girl that will live her life.
The Black girl that will not throw her gifts to the gators;
The Black girl that will one day be a wife.
The Black girl that will not forget who she is;
The Black girl that will help her country.
The Black girl that will not just write some checks;
The Black girl that will come back with the money.
The Black girl that will not leave her nation behind;
The Black girl that will wage war with her brain.
The Black girl that will never abandon the burden;
The Black girl that will no doubt make a change.
My Pearl is not just part of the treasure,
the real treasure is my Pearl.
The jewel is my mind & I'm different from all others.
I am not "A" Black girl, I am "the" Black girl.

What's Important

It can't be money because we stay broke.
It can't be a better tomorrow because we act like
there's no hope.
It can't be our people because we jump for the jobs
of service.
It can't be the families because we hurt members
that don't deserve it.
It can't be our society because in it genocide has
been carved.
It can't be our children because for some odd reason
we let them starve.
It can't be our daughters because if we have one we
it seems we never hold her.
It can't be our sons because we let villains walk in and turn
these young boys into Soldiers.
It can't be the village because armies march through & take.
It can't be the women because we don't defend
them, and they get raped.
It can't be the elders because often we neglect them.
It can't be natural resources because outsiders just
come and collect them.
It can't be the past because they tried to show us
the way.
It can't be the future because we didn't plant any
brand new seeds today.
Every Black Man in Africa needs to sit down and discuss
the position our beautiful continent is in
and everything that's important to us.

Whole Community

His siblings show him Brotherhood, bonding,
rivalry and being part of something larger.
His Father shows him safety, security, what
being a Man means.
Even what is required of him
mentally, physically, and spiritually.
His Mother introduces him to the world.
She shows him the difference between right and wrong.
She reveals what love and concern is.
also what manners, hygiene & respect are.
His teachers give him education and show him
technology.
His neighbors give him a sense of family out
side of the walls of home.
The store owners show him what bartering and trading is.
Plus, he sees what it means for something
to have value.
Workers around him show him skills, tools
diligence and sweating while getting a task done.
Fishermen show him patience and craftiness.
The Elders show him what wisdom, experience
and counsel looks like.
The religious give him a sense of something
spiritually greater than us.
The medicine Man or Doctor gives him a
peek into the workings of the body.
The Older Mothers show him obligation,
sensitivity, compassion, responsibility, and reward.

The Men show him strength, leadership, and duty.
The Women in general show him growth, change, beauty
virtue and commitment.
The children show him interaction, friendship,
sharing and competition.
The authorities show him law and boundaries.
He watches them all carefully.
Taking in the words, lessons, sights, and sounds
learning rapidly.
No one person can do this alone.
None of these titles by themselves can do what needs to be done
for his journey through life to be complete.
For him to reach his full potential.......???
It will take the Whole Community.

Black Hearted

I don't have any hidden animosity
but my thoughts and prayers extend to those that
grew up where I did.
I am extremely generous but
my arms open in the direction of family from the jump.
I am not stingy towards others but
my support goes to my people first.
I don't hate anyone but my initial
focus is on helping us.
I don't have any grievances to speak
of but my attention is on those that
look like me.
I have no grudges but my charity
applies to Mothers, Fathers, Sisters, and Brothers
of color.
I'm very giving but my humanitarianism
is spread out amongst those with pigment.
I don't disagree with anyone who doesn't have one but
my sympathy leans towards the darker faces.
My mind is on those that came from the
Motherland.
I am not racist, I am not a separatist
I am Black Minded and Black Hearted.

Our Ways

The rest of the world is growing
and we're shrinking.
Everyone else is starring into the future
and we're looking down and blinking.
Others are moving forward while we're
being left behind.
They're using, benefiting, and prospering from all the things
we never kept in mind.
All of them are going on being productive in society;
Saying we're wrong and being disruptive
but we never even try to be.
The rest of the population is living and we're
dying.
Everyone else is accepting, confessing, and
admitting but we're still denying.
Others are gaining momentum while we hesitate;
They manufacture and draft in experts
and we turn away the few we educate.
All of them continue to enjoy their years while we hate
the months, weeks, and days.
We'll start to make it better the very moment
we Change Our Ways

Iron Lady

It was her turn to exit the pearly gate
and she was born in Monrovia in 1938.
Optimistic about the world but there'd
be no celebration.
Until she accomplished her goal of getting
the best possible education.
Was always an over achiever but her
mind craved more.
And while the average person goes to one
College, she excelled in three or four
Traveled back to her home and became
a government official.
Then because of an army she had to run for
her life like a track star at the whistle.
Most of her colleagues got caught
and as a result were assassinated.
The nearest refuge was Kenya and while she
was there she just prayed and waited.
When the time came for the people to
once again make a selection.
Although hesitant, she returned and risked her neck for
Democracy in the election.
Taken into custody for simply
trying to do her best.
She conducted a pure and effective campaign
And ended up on "house arrest".
The "so-called" trial she was
given "under the law" would soon confirm her fears.
When it was said and done
she wasn't stunned, the verdict
was ten years.

She had served a short time
and then the next while.
They offered her a kind of physical freedom
if she'd go back into exile.
She left her home for the last time
but now hardened by the bricks.
And returned again to claim
the Presidency in the year 2006.
Earned her position and pushed
to be the one to get;
Labeled the first elected Female
Head of State on the entire continent.
She wanted to stop the violence
& taught that inside is where the origin of the cease lies.
In 2011 is when the world caught on to it
& decided to award her the Nobel Peace prize.
She became the pride of Liberia, & Africa, plus an
inspiration to Black people as a Whole.
Little Boys & Girls, Men & Women
of all colors across the globe.
Carrying the weight of a country
& being responsible for all of those lives daily.
Ellen Johnson Sirleaf—a leader, a sister,
a mother . . . The Iron Lady.

On The Blessing

I channel their resilience
and dare to picture success on the
playground of the most majestic animals.
I evoke every ounce of their collected strengths
and imagine a brighter future in the middle of
the most beautiful landscape.
I call forward a donation of wisdom from
each generation before me and dream dreams
of a better tomorrow on the spots of origin
for the Most ancient cultures.
I embody all that they were and envision
prosperity in the womb that first birthed
diamonds, gold & every other expensive thing
I am my ancestors and we are home.
They were, We are, I was;
Born on the Blessing.

When They Mention Me

In a place where the strong eat the weak.
Where the strong are the meek.
No doubt being able to physically take lives
is only half the battle.
Having left the lives you've killed to protect;
ALONE… wandering and starving like cattle.
Not being able to say, "I really led the ones
that followed me;"
Not providing food, supplies, education
or technology.
Trying to do the right thing but spilling blood
on the whim;
When murdering "their" people like they murder
"your" people makes you no better than them.
If I could be in that position– I'd make
Sure that when they mention me;
They'll say I dragged my kinsmen from
war in the past, to peace in this century.

Growling

Killing our chance at growing by not feeding the brain.
Pride keeps us from acknowledging
how enticing the menu is.
Ignoring "the truth" that books are delicious.
Denying the fact that what's on the plate
smells inviting.
It's unimaginable that we are deaf to the
vocalization of it's displeasure.
We try our best to ignore what it needs
but it was designed to be fed daily.
Hunger pains announce themselves and we
think we show strength by not taking heed
to the rumbling.
Losing mental weight for not putting something
in it and watching satisfaction arrive on
the other faces after they've had their fill.
Witnessing the malnutrition wreak havoc on
each individual that chooses not to raise the
fork to the brows.
Seeing the deterioration of the people from
not lifting the spoon between the ears.
Not refueling the tank is death's invitation.
We must listen to the echo of emptiness.
Our Minds Are Growling.

A New Day

The Black people of the past are disappearing.
No more taking the backseat.
No more neglecting our needs all to be favored.
The Black people of old are disappearing.
Not hating each other and working together.
Not taking the easy way out and handling business.
The Black people of those years are disappearing.
Unaware of the capabilities of the enemy.
Blind to the craftiness of the opposition.
The Black people of yesterday are disappearing.
Uneducated and ignorant.
Allowing our people to suffer degradation
Those people are almost gone
and they will not return.
The ones that will and have emerged from
those ashes love one another.
This generation is proud of who they are,
proud of what they look like,
and optimistic about the future.
It's a New Day.

Men

We are the beginning.
Continuation rests with us.
The family takes a seat on our shoulders.
Not the word, but the meaning;
of security, of safety, of togetherness.
Of love and being part of a unit.
Our responsibility is the generation
the name, bloodline, the road, the flag
and the land.
We are the record keepers of time
and history.
The past is our treasure and demands restoration.
It is our nourishment and relief.
We are the protectors of the Elder,
the Wife and the Child.
We are the flag bearers of the skin,
race, and color.
Servants of the village, town, city, or
Community.
We are the physically stronger half
They call us, Men.

Our President

African and American.
He operated with in impunity in the community.
was loved by the children and adults.
Heard their complaints and moved to get them results.
Instantly found himself on the fast track to this.
Title, position, and recognition as an activist
From the Illinois Senate to a US senator for years
Earned the respect of his constituents and peers.
Three universities including Harvard Law,
are the colleges that got his foot in the door.
Then before he could blink he was shown his better half,
and became a professor and lawyer that married a lawyer and more.
Those who knew him best felt the way he
drew people to him was evidence; he
could do what hadn't been done and make a
strong candidate for the presidency.
Him conducting a campaign that was clean
showed the entire world the one thing they had never seen.
He chose to fight the war with his brain
and overcame shame, taunts, and slander about his name.
The two daughters watched their parents
and were proud of them both.
The win was solidified on 1-20-09 as he took the oath
He then gave us the only first lady who was born a Cherub.
In return was labeled one, like there was
something wrong with being an Arab
Head-on is how the problems were met
Never once did they ever see him sweat
From a little boy in Hawaii playing in dirty shoes,

To a grown Man running for office showing all thirty-two's
Humbly moved onto the scene,
became the living breathing dream of Dr. King.
Using his words as his dominion,
Completing the race like a true Kenyan.
Honesty got him a connection,
But quitting smoking helped him capture the election.
Making it over every obstacle,
Allowing his life to become the impossible.
Held on to his family in the midst of the drama.
Barack had no idea that he'd evolve into O'Bama
Never even realizing that he later would
Give up all of his privacy for the greater good.
As a Son he cared about the poor, wasn't on
the take and would rather GIVE
and is Remembered as the undisputed coolest
commander in chief that ever lived.
He was Hated on but wasn't hesitant.
Accomplished much although the blocking was evident
One Black Man . . . One World Resident;
Our Brother, Our Leader, Our President

Bless Haiti

Lord I know you see Haiti. Your people.
A giving people. A hospitable people. Submerged in family.
Their lives have been affected in a mighty tragic way
and we ask that you put a fence around their spirits.
Protect them Lord. Give them Peace of Mind. Drive
despair, confusion, doubt, and quitting far from them.
You said, "No weapon formed against us shall prosper
and every tongue that rises up against us in judgment;
We would condemn. Right now Lord a weapon has been
formed and executed against the people of Haiti but
we know that it did not and will not prosper. It was
sent to put out the flame that is the will of the people
themselves, but the enemy is a liar! Even though he
desires to sift them as wheat, they will recover!
They will rebuild. They will be stronger, wiser people, and a
better nation when this is over.
Many that didn't know you, will after this. We ask that you show
them the mercy only you can and forgive not only
them for their sins but all of us for our sins.
Give us all a mind to turn and walk the straight
and narrow. Protect us all Lord and let your
will be done. In Jesus's name, Amen.

That Place

Where my skin doesn't offend
and my hair doesn't scare.
Where I don't look outta place
and every face resembles my face.
Black, classy, and can afford to be;
Maintaining the space of the Majority.
Where the atmosphere is peaceful and orderly;
and education is a priority.
Where all privileges reach small villages.
Where all shades are treated equal
and the heroes on tv are my people.
Where ALL and not some of these;
are totally African Companies.
Where the Woman and the Girl are safe;
from torture, assault, murder and rape.
Where every single child has a chance;
to study, learn, play, and dance.
Where I can take a deep breath, relax, and savor;
the fact of having a home with a next-door neighbor.
Where presence, effort and time are mine to give.
This is where I dream one day I'll live.

Imagine

Imagine as a Parent having to wake your daughter or son
Holding on to them tightly while you & your companion run
Imagine my country being so poor and
not having the money to hire;
and as a result of being overrun by militia that
learns to earn with guns and fire.
Executing the old and kidnapping the young;
Amputating body parts, extinguishing life
and leaving none.
Brutalizing Women and Girls that are
dying trying to escape.
Because homes are gone, families are dead
and they refuse to choose slavery or rape.
Imagine them sparing my hide, if I select to join the evil.
or imagine me getting shot down because I'm not the type
to ever betray my people.
Imagine building a house with your bare hands
& outback planting vegetables row by row
Working hard as possible by day & at night having
somewhere safe for your family to go. Imagine only owning
a little bit but being patient until you can earn something
more. Imagine seeing the same drive, determination
& work ethic from the people that live next door
Now imagine hundreds of angry soldiers
relentlessly storming your village
Invading homes, murdering everyone with all intent to pillage.

Melting Pot

I can't be colorblind, till I find which color's mine.
Salvaging culture lost, that'll only be regained through time.
Results of crimes against our bodies and minds;
that we've adopted and directed to be passed down the line.
The harmonies of bad habits ring as chimes.
Hurt and pain remain because we're trained to
ignore the signs.
I can't love and get along with anyone else;
Until I check the mirror, know who I am,
being proud and content with myself.
Jumping down from the shelf that comes with wealth.
Licks that hit like bricks
and whelps from persuasive belts
Admiring the ones that stood strong, realizing the good's gone
The one's experiencing what I've felt
and finally learning to play the hand we've been dealt
The piercing rays of sunshine all in one mind
The single thing making ice between us melt

Our Leader

Angelic hands chose his Father and whom he'd be
kin to
The worthy one was the Paramount Chief of the
Thimbu
It was beyond what they thought they knew or what
they'd think
and He showed up in 1918, in July on the 18th
Grew too fast and saw peace was too far in the
distance
So he helped respond to apartheid with armed
resistance
Encouraging all the people by telling them that they
can be
A member of the new youth league called the
A.N.C
Went underground to size up the situation
Led the organization of the Spear of the Nation
Charged with capital offenses in 1963
In 64 sentenced to prison for L-I-F-E.
Suffering in a place comparable to Hades
Locked up through the end of the '60s to the
beginning of the '80s
Never wrote in the script, that it would cost this in the plan
but after his release appointed to the highest
office in the land
A long life and the Nobel Peace Prize for all to see
them
Forever a symbol of reconciliation and freedom
His story is motivation for the hearts and eyes of any
reader
He is Nelson Mandela, Madiba, Our leader

Black Male

He is unmarked envelopes that are justification
for me paying for my violations to remain hidden.
He is bills passed in the dark that rightfully
accuse me of my wrongdoing
and when paid allow it all to stay secret.
He is empty bank accounts that show accountability for sins
I've kept under lock and key.
He is numbers transferred to other numbers and
the reason I'm held responsible for these hidden atrocities.
He is deadlines met in secluded places that explain
why I've received a lesser sentence and why my deeds remain buried.
He is debts decreased in shadows and is the
core of my pleading the fifth.
This rotation prevents embarrassing things
from becoming public knowledge.
He is knots of green paper left in strange places
and the ball and chain that forces me to reimburse
some of what I've forcefully taken from the helpless.
He is lump sums exchanging hands preventing
the shattering of my façade.
Without action, everyone will know my lie.
He is why my past will always be my present.
He is the haunting act trying not to act like an enemy.
He can only feel animosity towards me for
getting away with all that I have.
I must make "whistle blowing" a shameful thing.
I must make his allegations for their reparations a crime
I speak of the Black Male.

About the Author

With more poetry, novels, children's books, highly opinionated scripts, spiritual texts, how-tos, and even a cookbook, Robert Davis is a longtime author of twelve more (and counting) soon to be published literary works to his credit. Eager to feed the masses, he aims to be one of the most seasoned and widely ranged talents of his generation. His passions include public speaking, art, music, reading, movies, cooking, exercise, teaching, and family. Plus, He is very active in his church & community. He is also the president of a record label, and in his lifetime, he has founded several local grassroots organizations in Jackson, Mississippi, where he currently resides.

CPSIA information can be obtained
at www.ICGtesting.com
Printed in the USA
BVHW051728160622
639961BV00009B/432